T O A D

Art Director: Rita Marshall
Book Design: Stephanie Blumenthal
Text Adapted and Edited from the French language by Kitty Benedict
Library of Congress Cataloging-in-Publication Data
Benedict, Kitty.
Toad/written by Andrienne Soutter-Perrot; adapted for the American reader
by Kitty Benedict; illustrated by Monique Felix.
Summary: Discusses the physical characteristics, habits, and natural
environment of the toad.
ISBN 0-88682-568-7
1. Toads—Juvenile literature. [1. Toads.]
I. Soutter-Perrot, Andrienne. II. Felix, Monique, ill. III. Title.
QL668.E227B46 1992
597.8'7--dc20   92-14165

TOAD

WRITTEN BY

ANDRIENNE SOUTTER-PERROT

ILLUSTRATED BY

MONIQUE FELIX

CREATIVE EDUCATION

WHAT IS IT?

Is it a frog? Not at all! It is a great big toad, crouching beneath a rock.

It sits very still, its hind legs bent into a Z. Its front legs are spread far apart.

With its round, gold eyes, it watches everything that moves. It can hear the faintest sounds, such as the hum of a bee's wings.

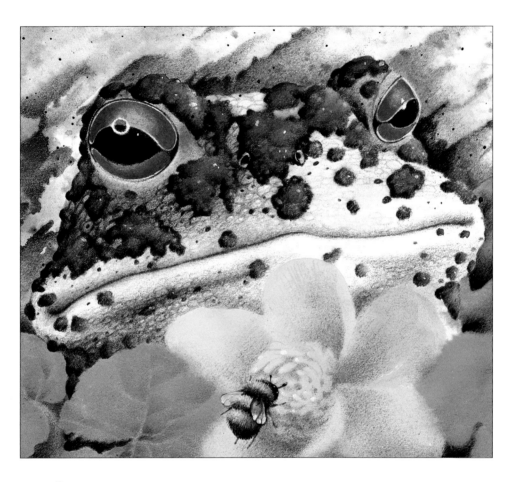

It breathes through two small nostrils, smelling all the nearby odors. A wide mouth stretches across its face.

WHERE DOES IT LIVE?

The toad doesn't like the hot sun, so it stays
hidden all day in a cool, damp spot.

The toad breathes partially through its skin, which must stay cool and moist in order to let in oxygen from the air.

When the sun sets, the toad slowly starts out from its hiding place.
It must hunt for its food.

The toad may be slow, but if it is frightened, it can hop away fast.

If the toad sees a moving insect or worm, it stays very still.

Suddenly the toad flicks out its long, sticky tongue, catching the insect or worm and pulling it back into its mouth. It swallows its prey whole because it has no teeth.

The toad may eat up to four of these meals on a summer night.

In fall and winter, the toad stops eating. It huddles alone in a hole, safe from storms and cold.

HOW DO TOADS REPRODUCE?

In the spring all toads—first the males, then the females—come out of hiding. They gather by the hundreds in swamps and ponds.

Soon the toads mate. A male mounts a female's back, embracing her with his front legs.

This embrace continues for several days as the female lays her
eggs—thousands of little black balls covered with clear jelly.

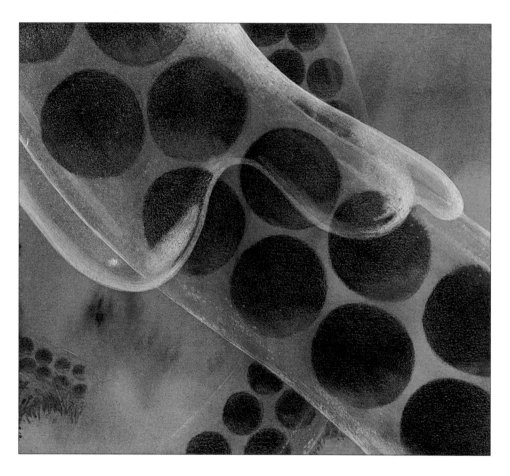

The male toad sprays the eggs with a colorless liquid that contains sperm. This is how the eggs are fertilized.

The female toad weaves the eggs in long ribbons around water plants.

The male and female toads then leave the pond, going their separate ways.

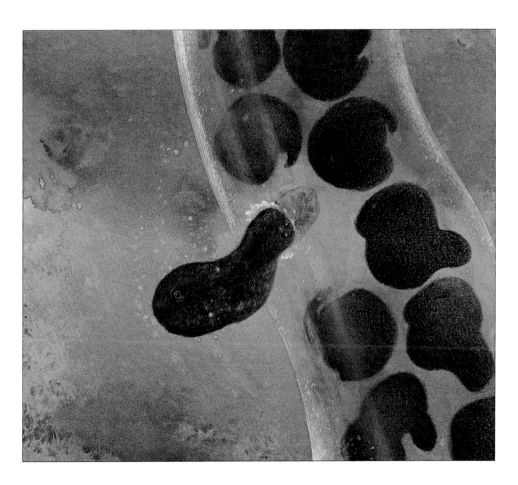

A few days later, a tiny black tadpole wiggles out of the clear jelly surrounding an egg.

The tadpole swims like a fish, feeding on plants and breathing oxygen from the water.

Soon four small feet emerge on the tadpole, and little by little its tail begins to disappear.

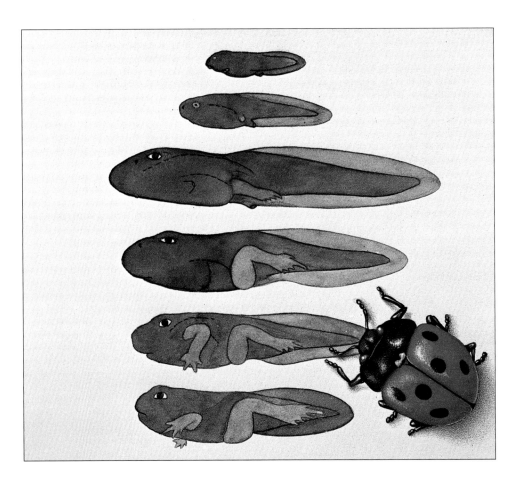

This change from tadpole to toad is called a metamorphosis.

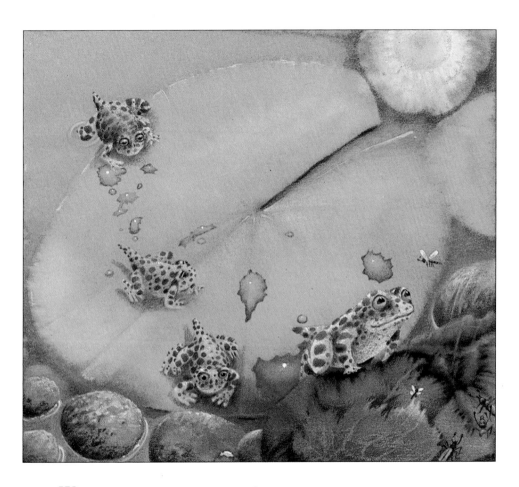

When the metamorphosis is complete, the little toad is about an inch long. It leaves the water and hops onto dry land. It eats gnats, flies, ants, and aphids.

The toad will keep growing for several years. Then it will return to the water to spawn its own young.

HOW DO TOADS HELP US?

Animals such as toads, frogs, and lizards, who live part of their lives in water and part on land, are called amphibians.

Toads eat many insects that are harmful to plants. Tadpoles and baby toads also serve as food for many other animals.

But the toads don't eat all the insects, and not all baby toads are eaten. Just the right amount of each is left.

Toads are an important part of nature's cycle. We should be happy to see toads in our gardens.